Cultural Arts in Columbus Book Series Vol 2

Murals and Street Arts in Columbus Ohio
Part 1 Short North and Downtown

Shoichiro Nakamura

Printed by CreateSpace, Sold at Amazon.com
Published in 2017
ISBN-13:978-1546559993

Preface

Columbus city is decorated with many art works such as mural and sculptures. Murals and sculptures in public view brighten the street, give joy to the pedestrians and welcome visitors. Murals and sculptures in the street are often humorous but have historical values, too. Columbus is fortunate also by having many buildings that have art works inside which can be seen by public. Some of those arts are even visible from the street through glass windows. Many galleries in Columbus show art works. Even private stores are decorated with art works entertaining their customers as well as pedestrians.

This book is to capture some of these arts in photos. It is hoped that another book will be able to cover more arts on the street. The photos in this book will be available in the forms of greeting card or larger print as written more in details at the end of this book.

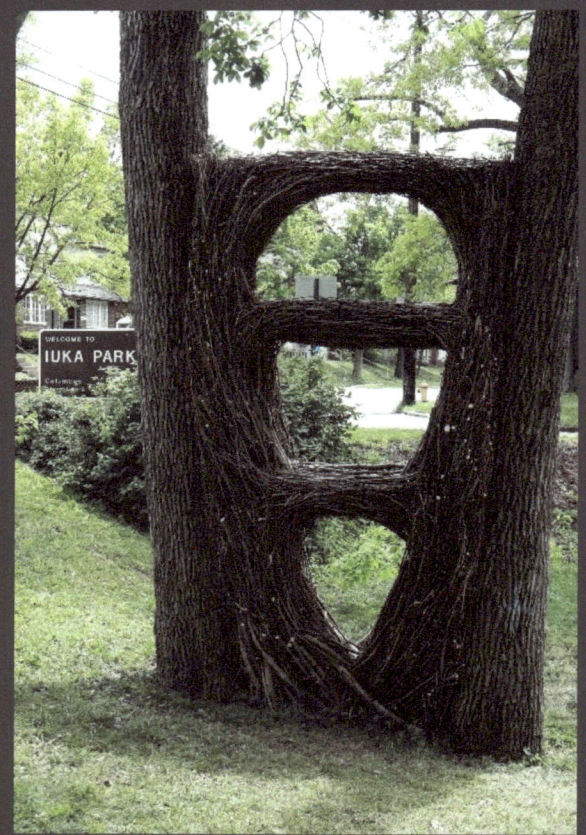

Wood sculpture in Iuka Park between
Summit St and N Fourth St

OSU Gateway
North High Street

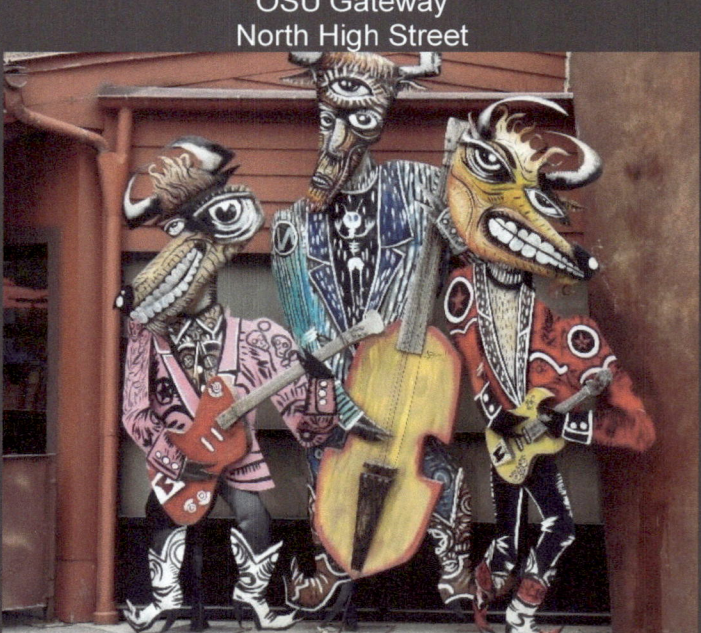

Italian Village
N Sixth St and Detroit Ave

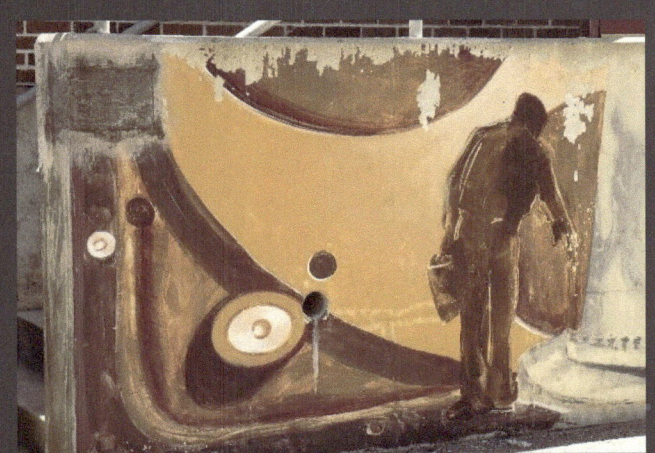
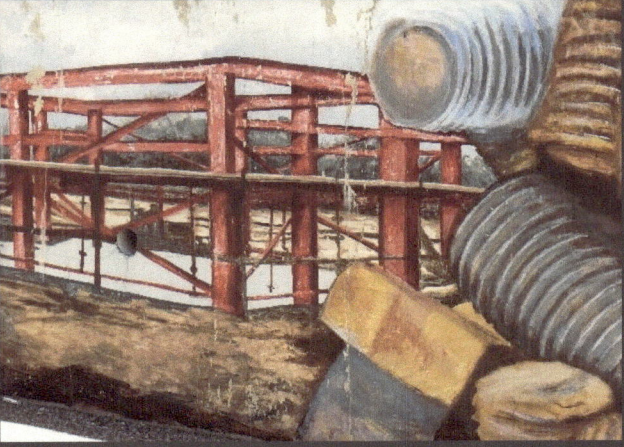
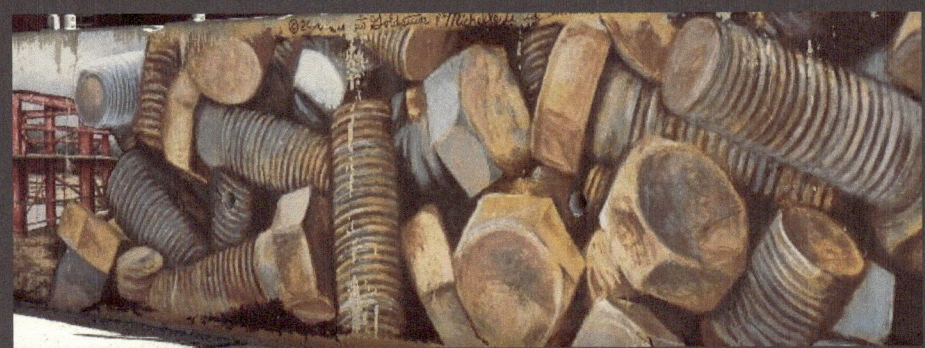
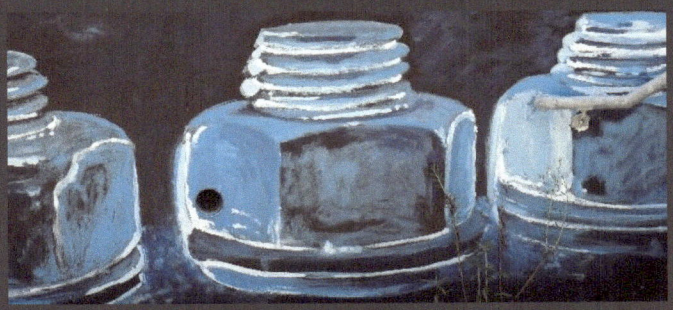

Short North along N High St

Mural by Erick Rausch and Jen Kiko
Third floor in Goodale Parking Garage, north of Convention Center

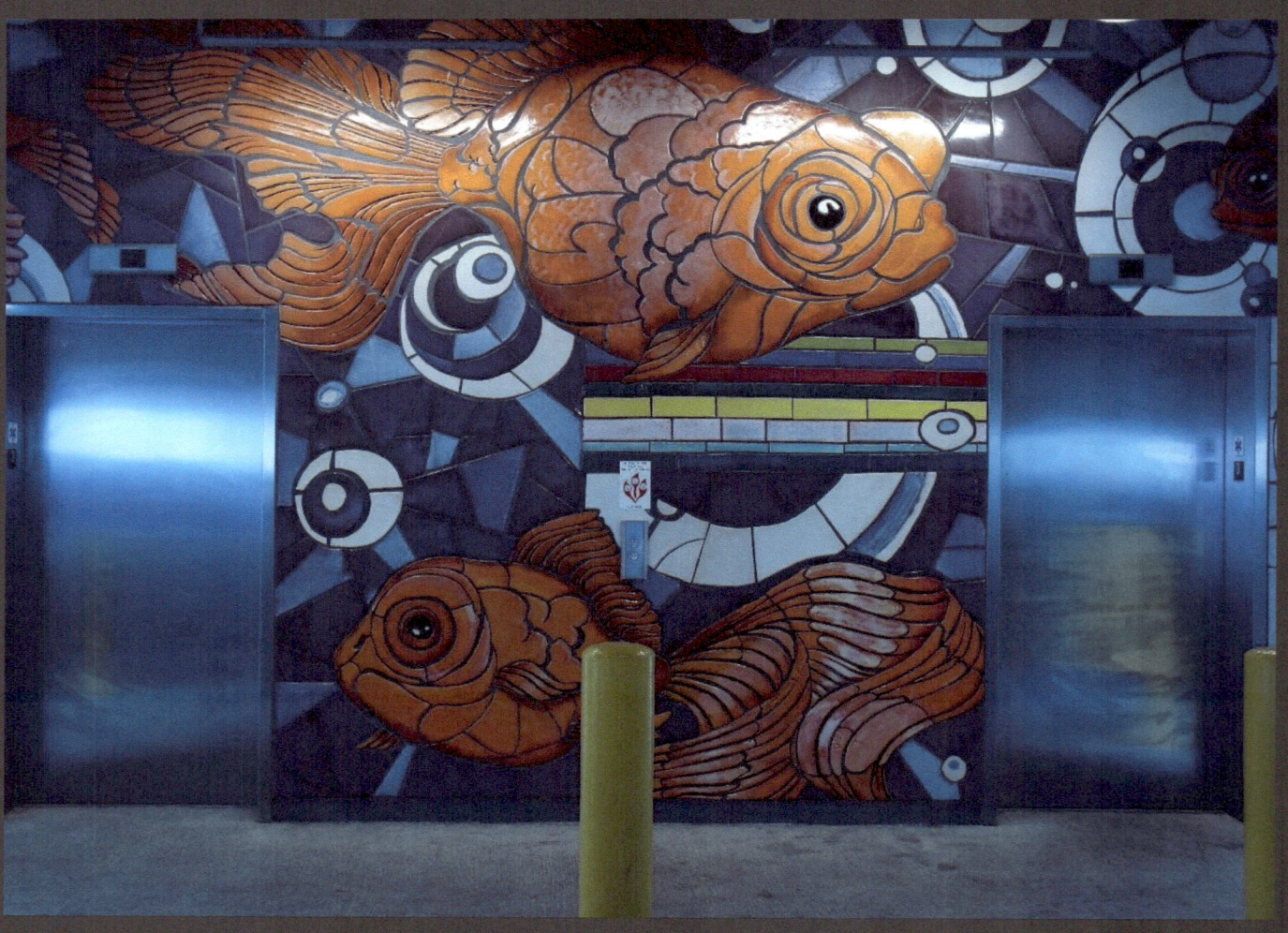

Mural by Erick Rausch and Jen Kiko, North High St and E Fifth Ave

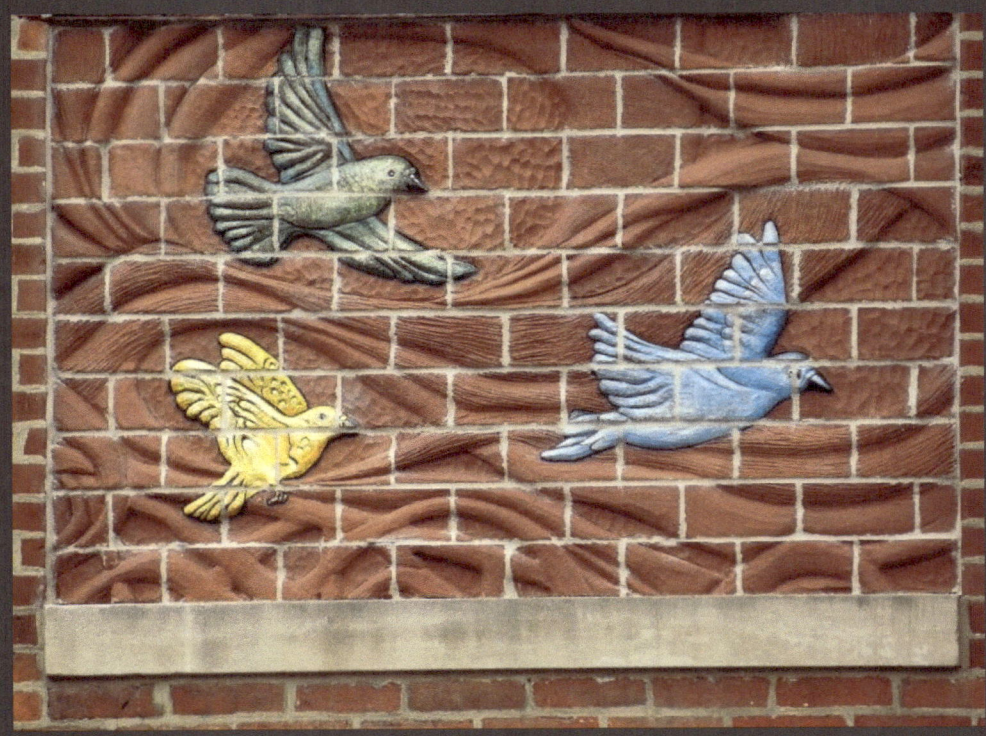

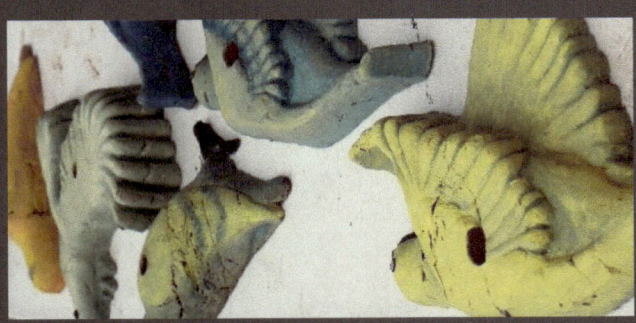

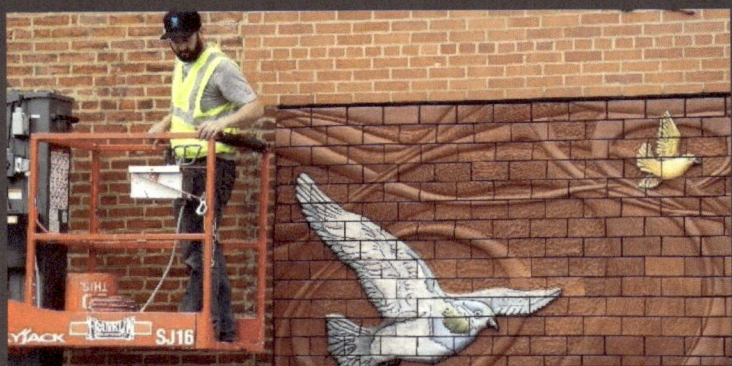

Murals along N High Street in Short North

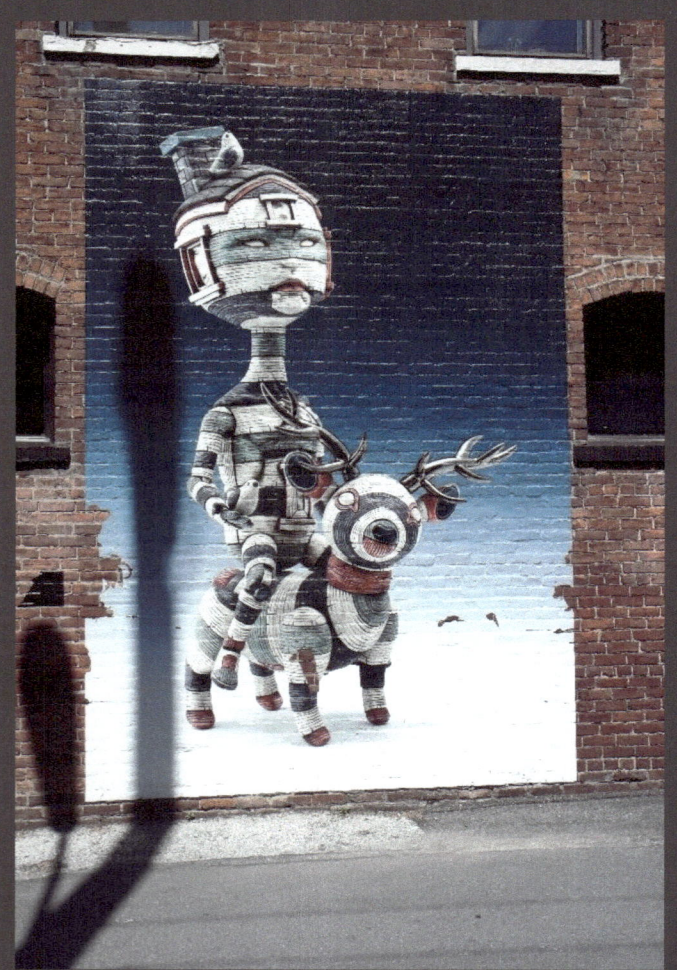

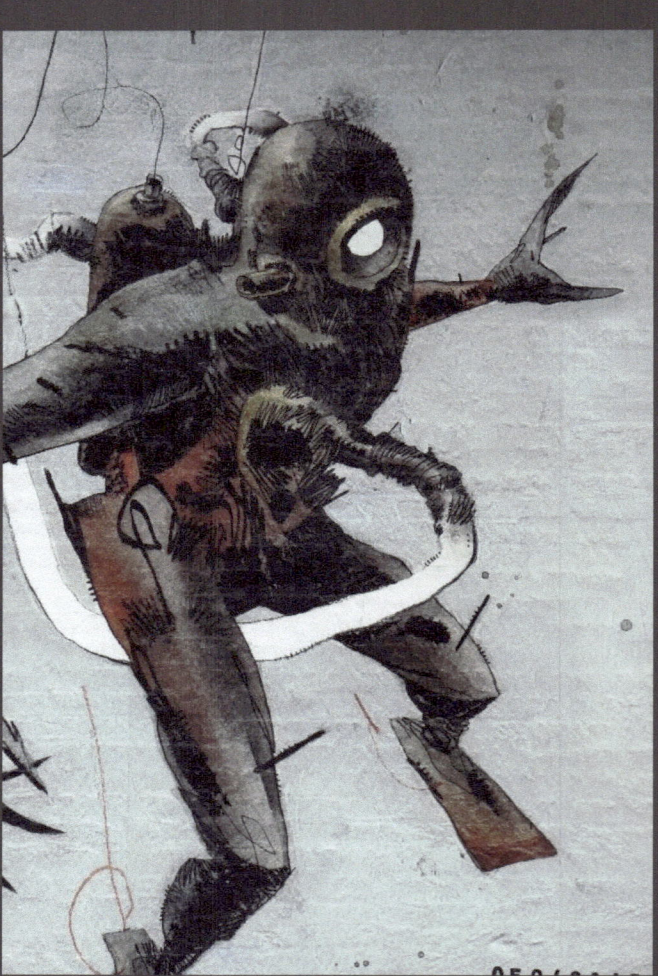

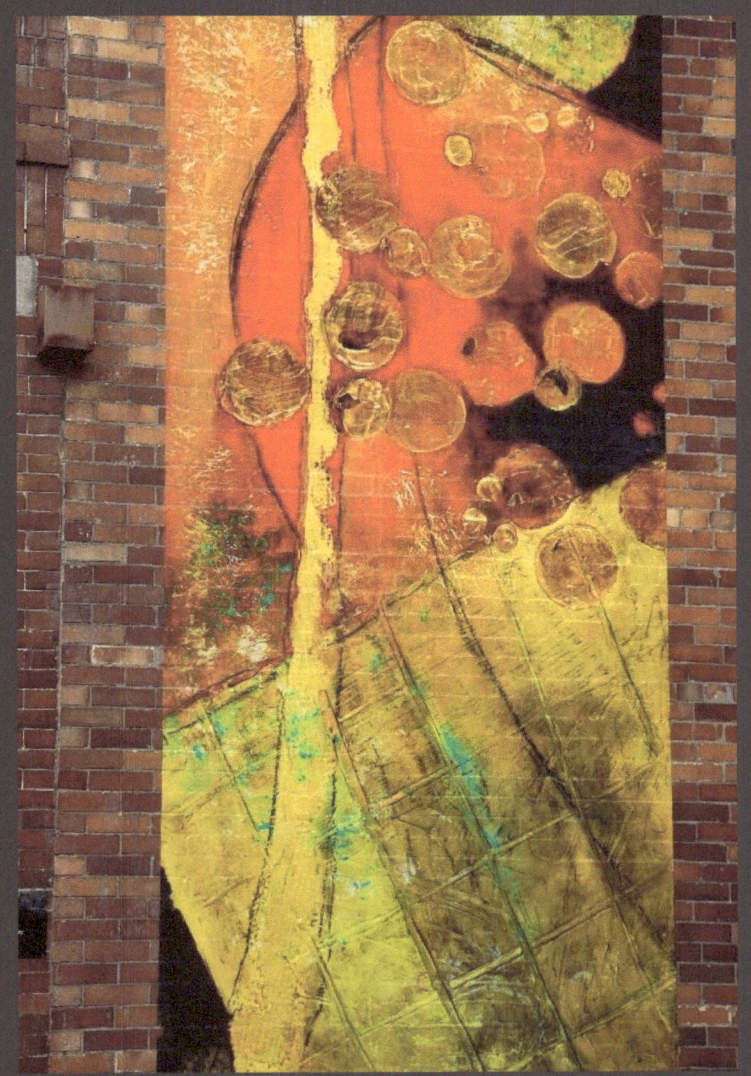 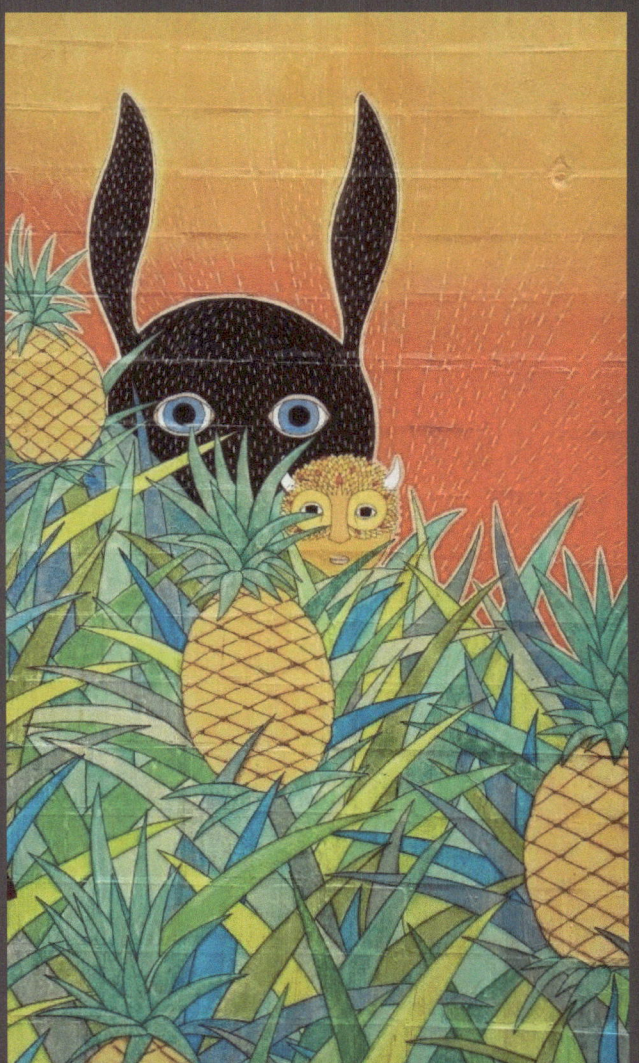

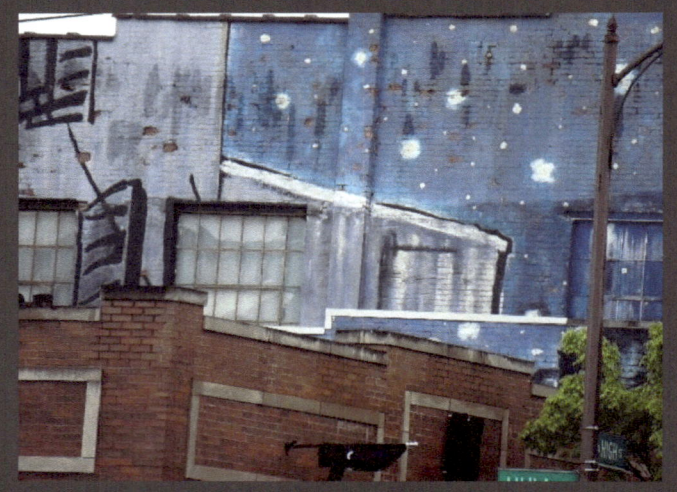

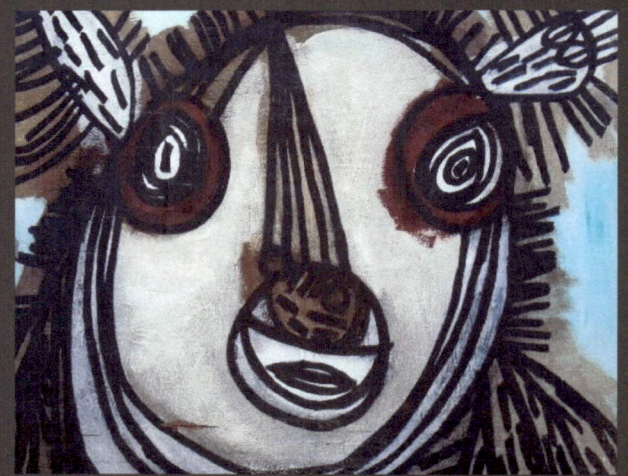

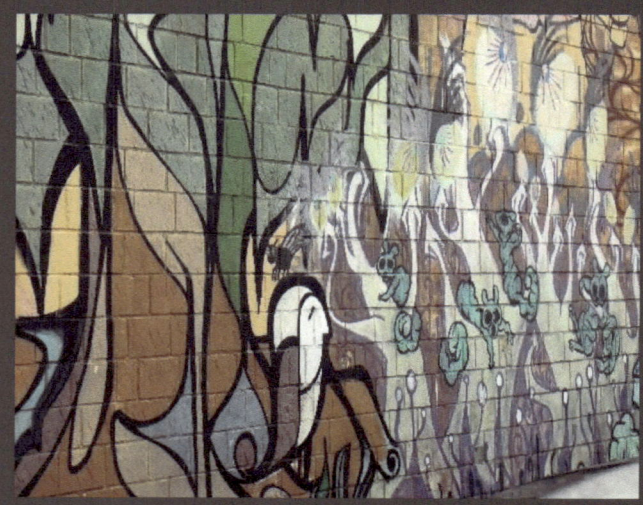

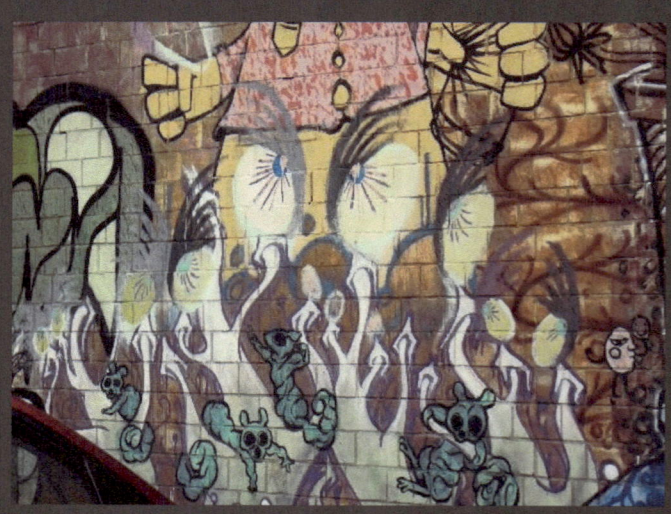

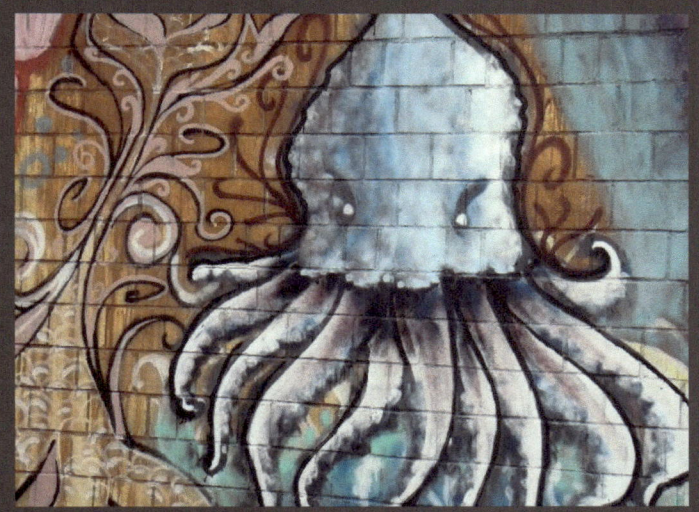

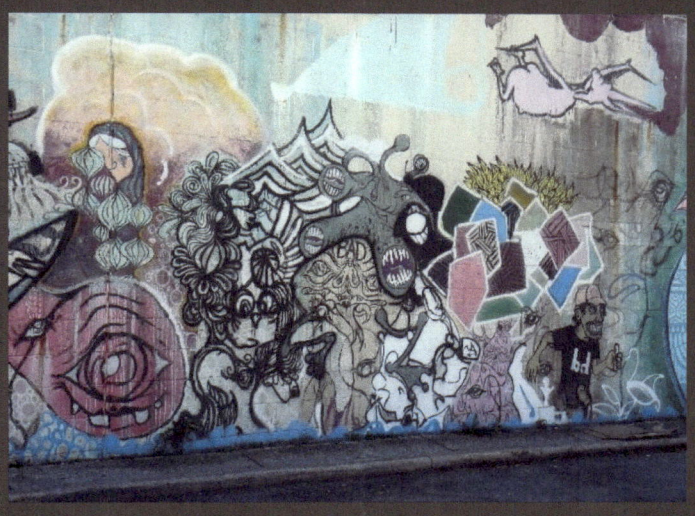

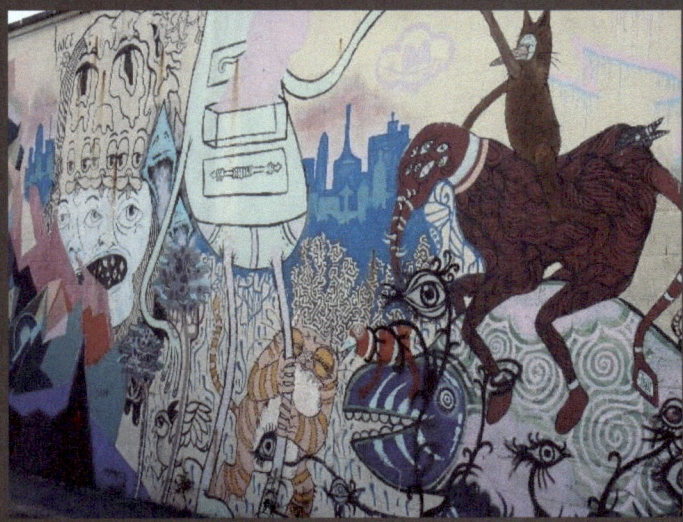

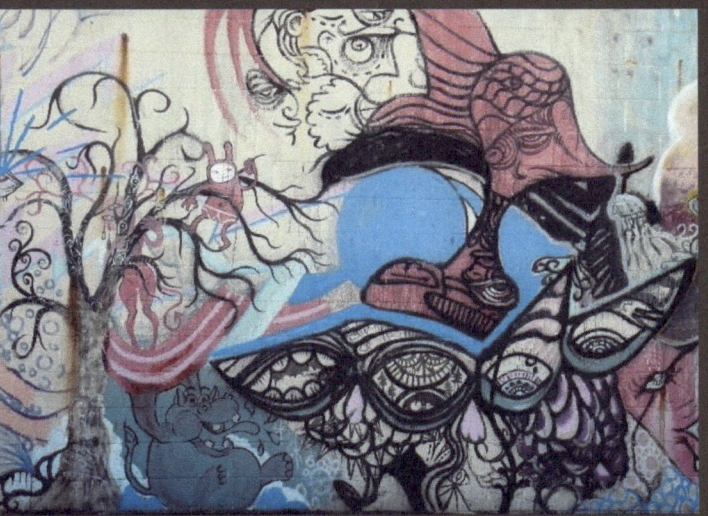

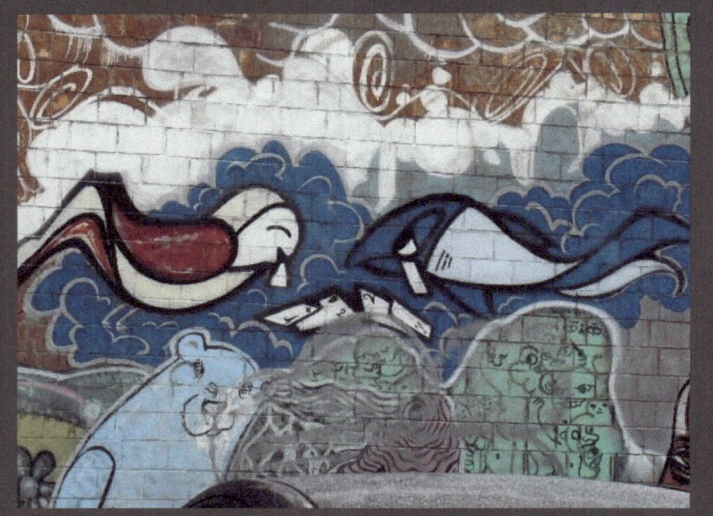

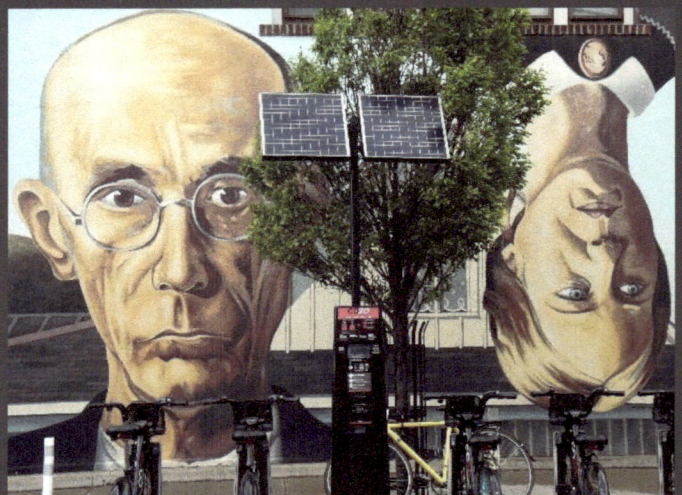

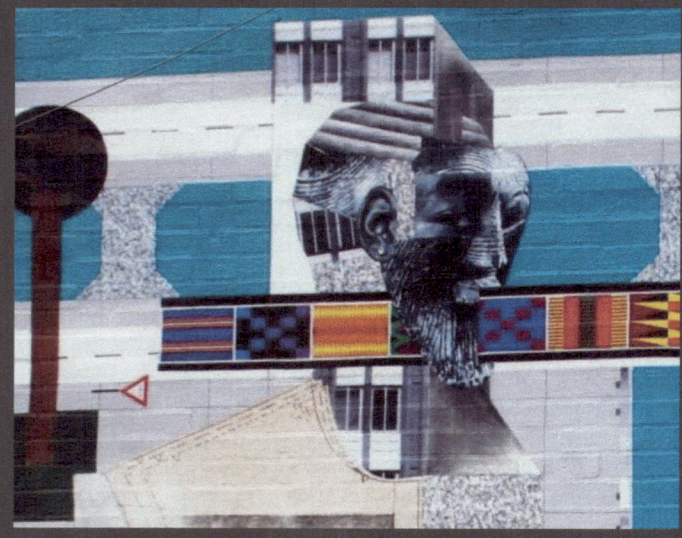

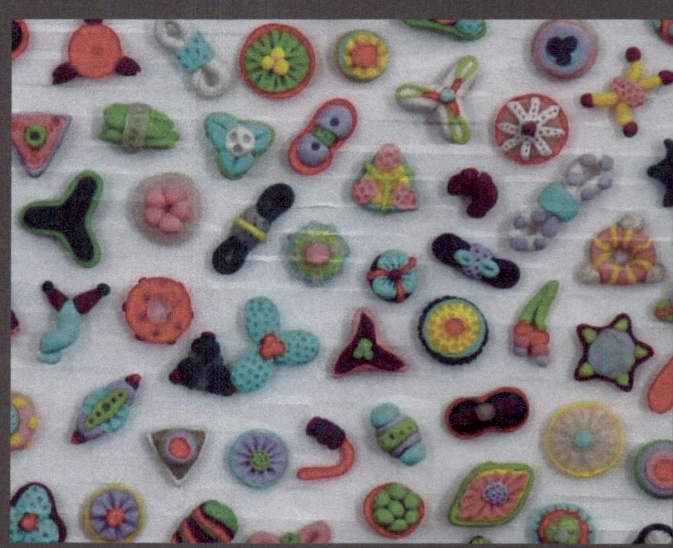

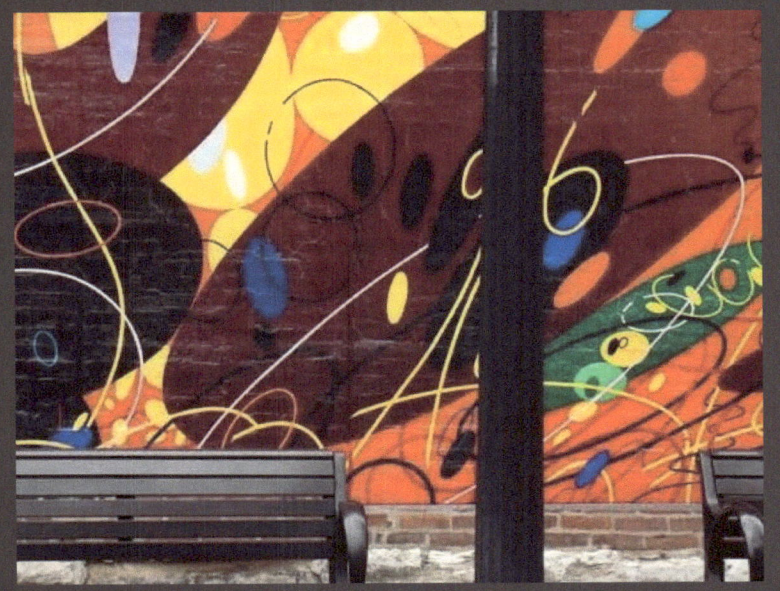

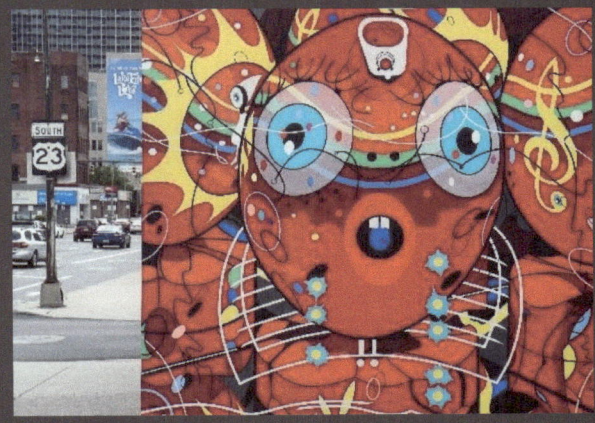

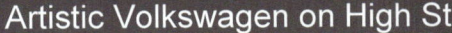
Artistic Volkswagen on High St

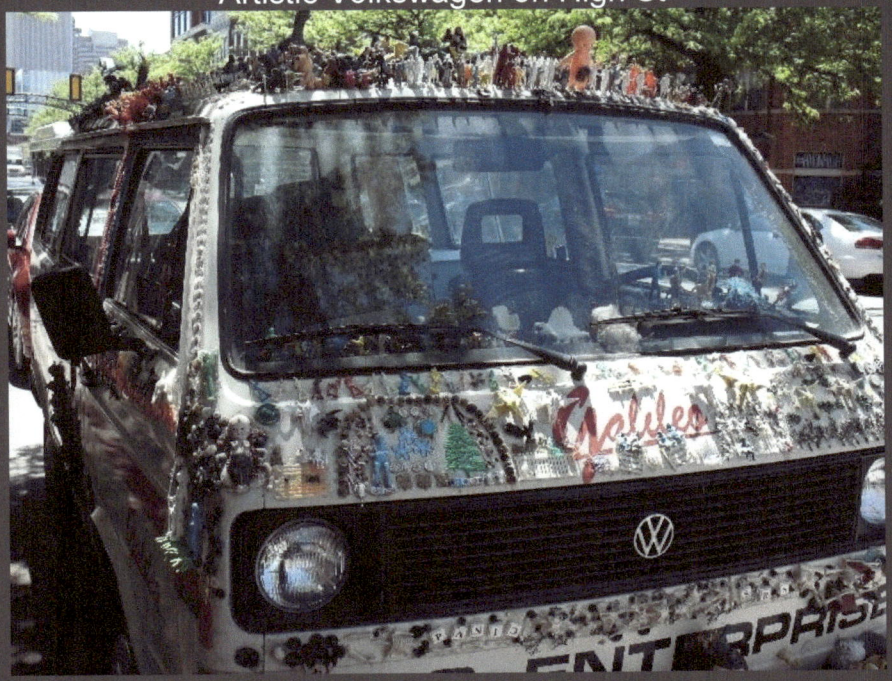

Inside Convention Center

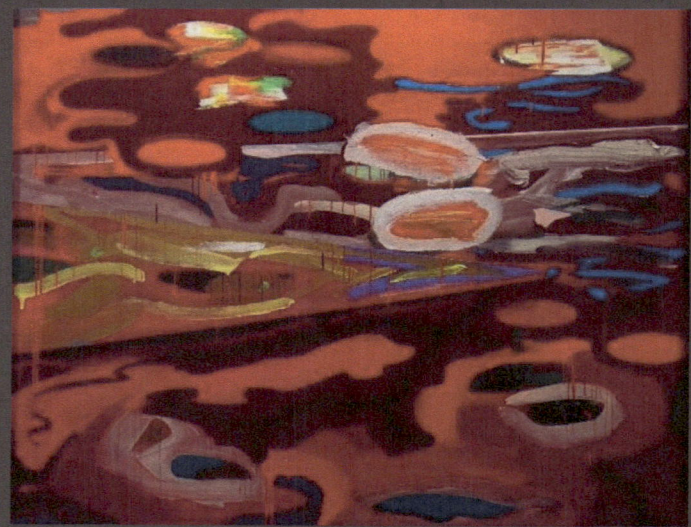 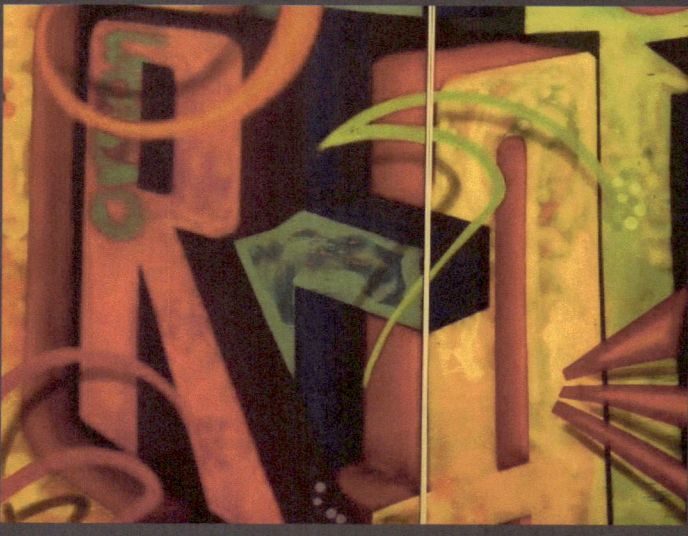

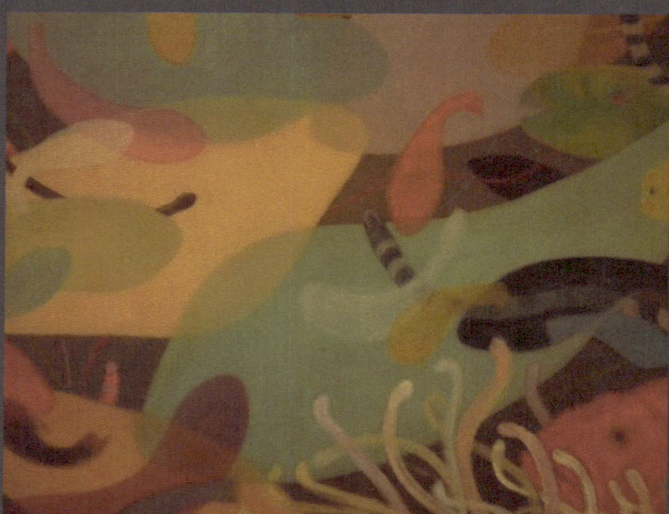 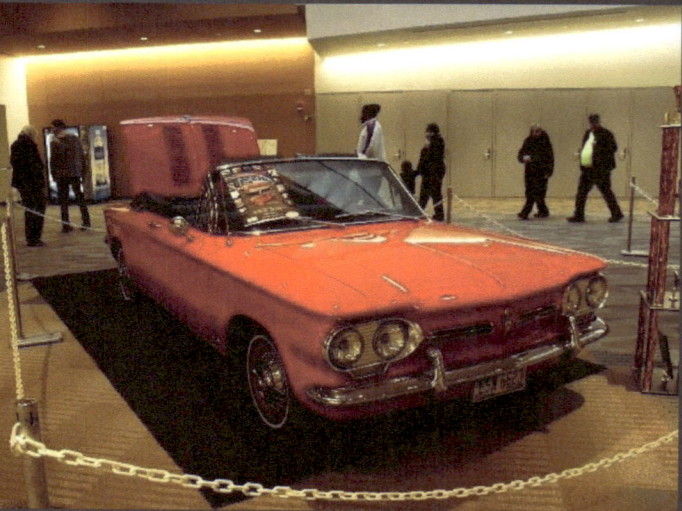

(Above right:Antique GM Corvair displayed in Convention Center Downtown Columbus)

Metal sculpture in front of Hilton Downtown Columbus

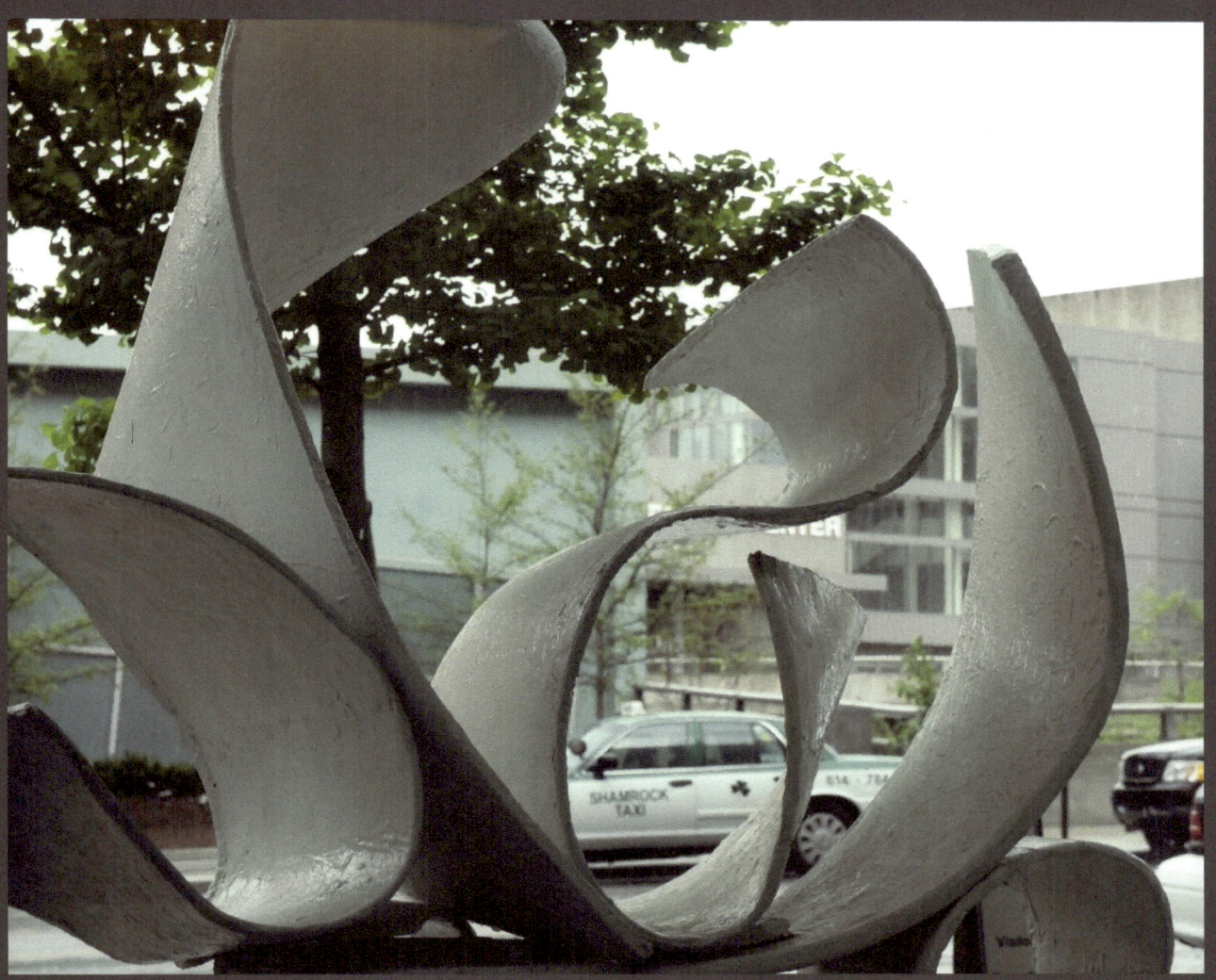

Sculpture in the front yard of Pizzuti Collection Museum along Park St north of Goodale St

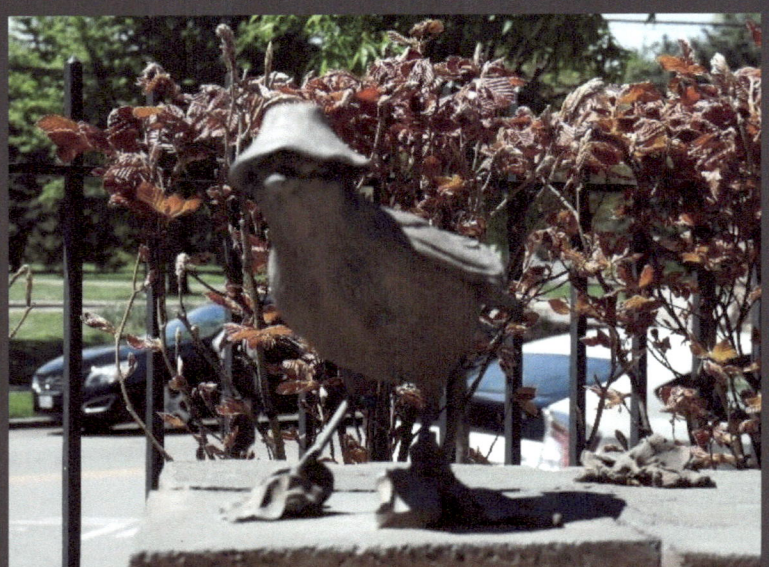
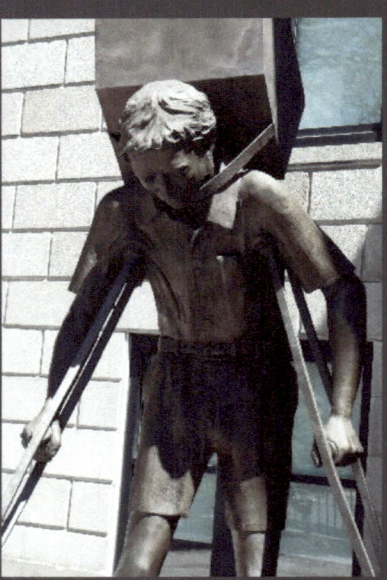

Please do not urinate in public view
Front yard of Pizzuti Collection Museum along Park St near Goodale Park

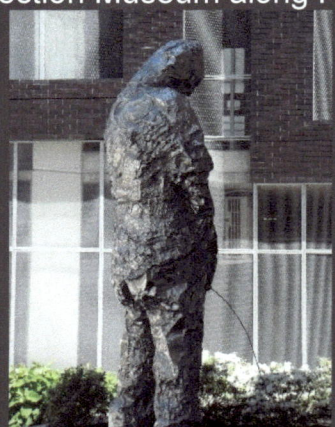

Sculpture inside Anthropologies, an apparel store, in Short North

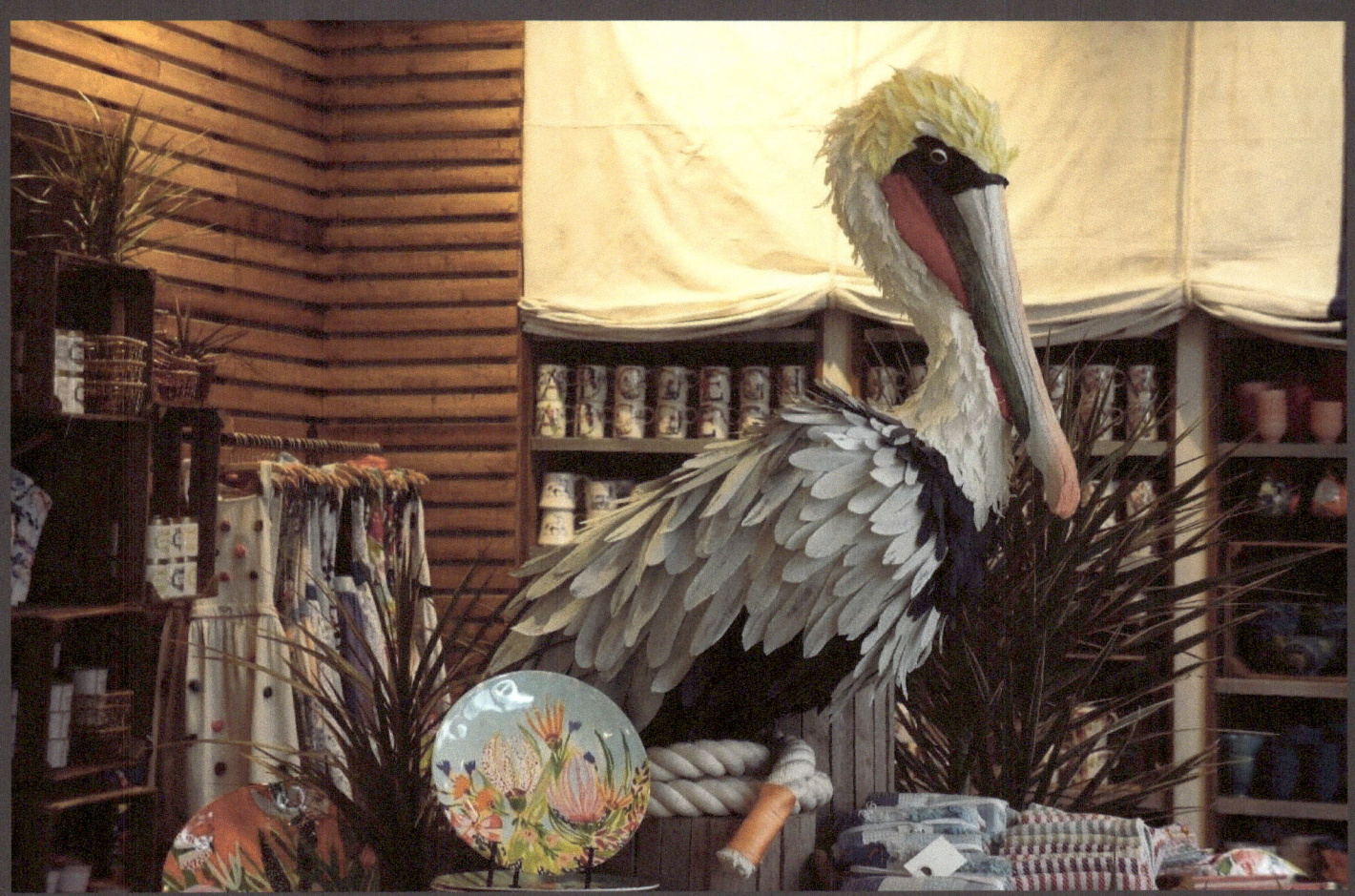

South of Broad St
Near Federal Building along S Civic Center Dr

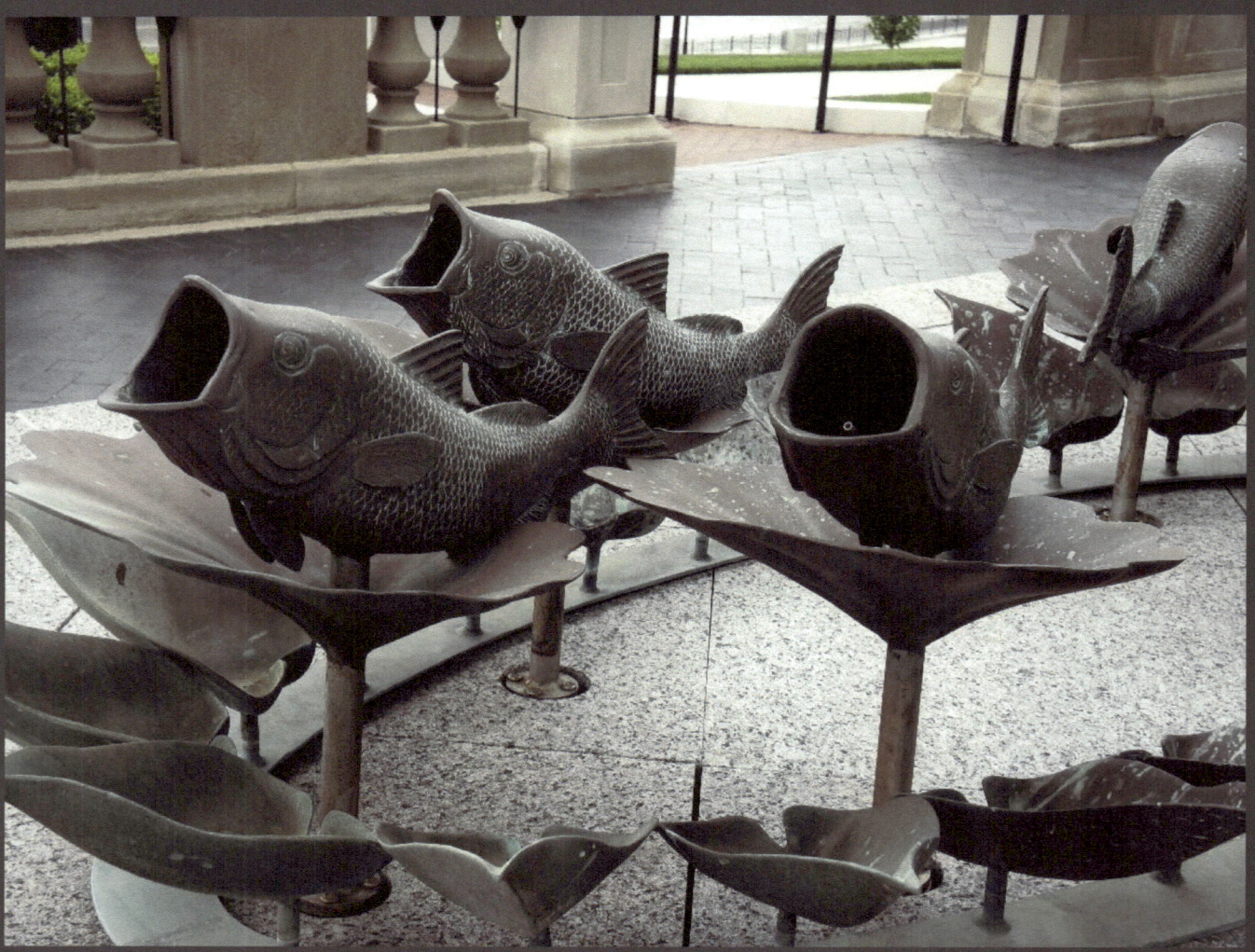

Looking through the window at S Civic Center Dr and W Rich St

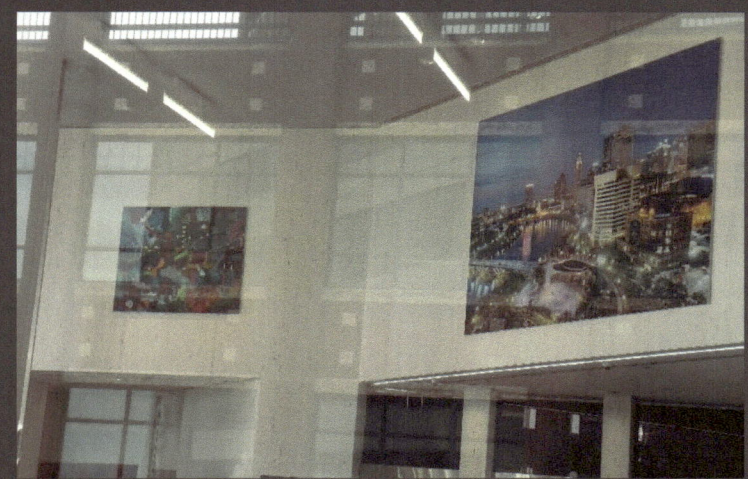
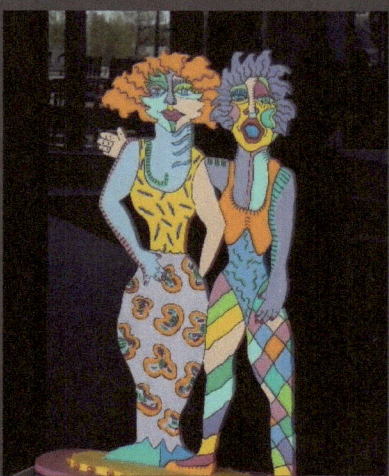
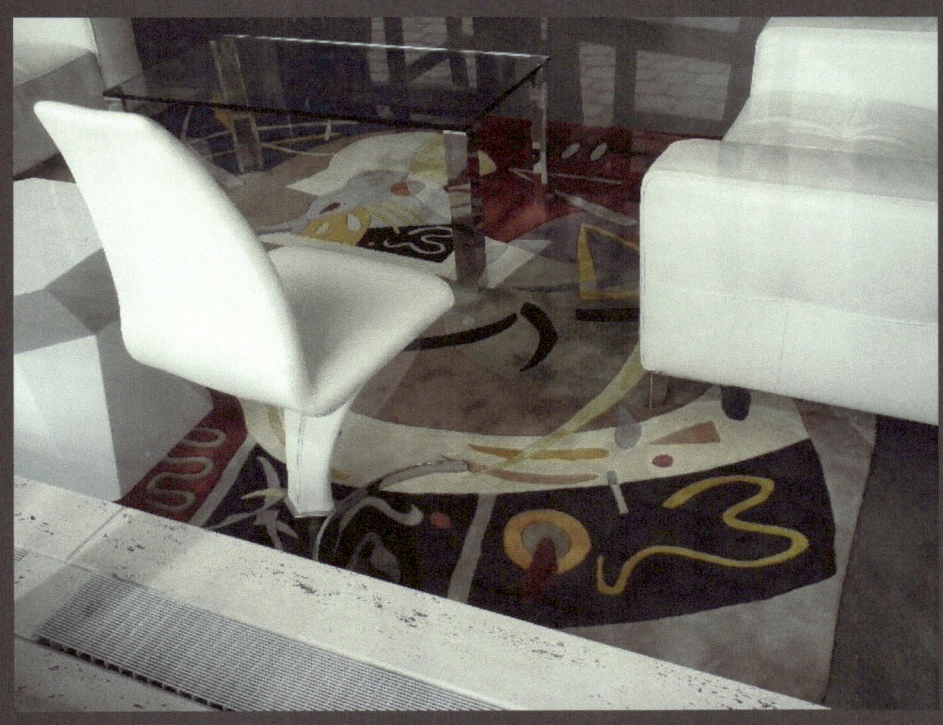

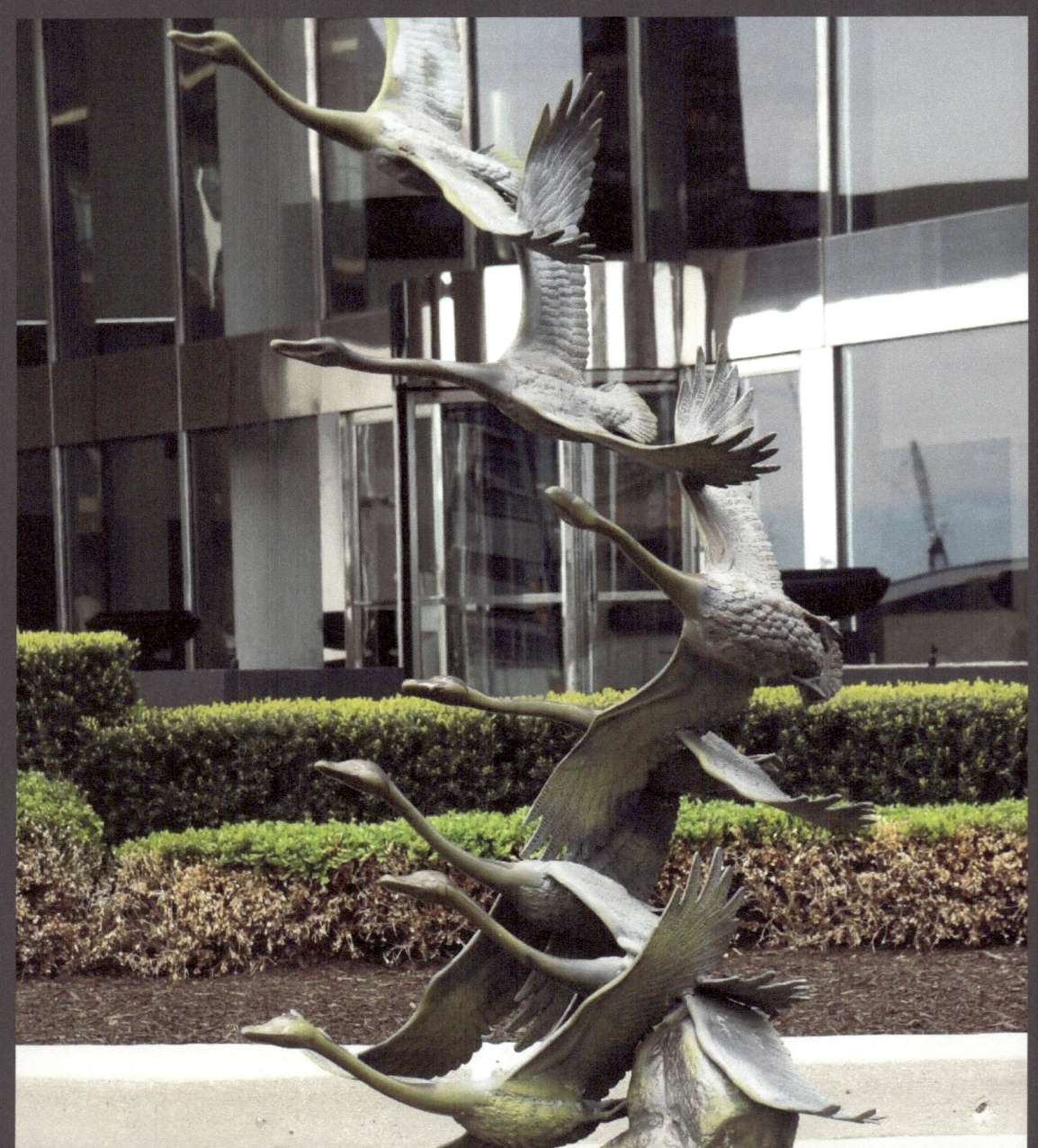

Civic Center Dr
and
W Rich St

Murals at S Pear St & E Mound St

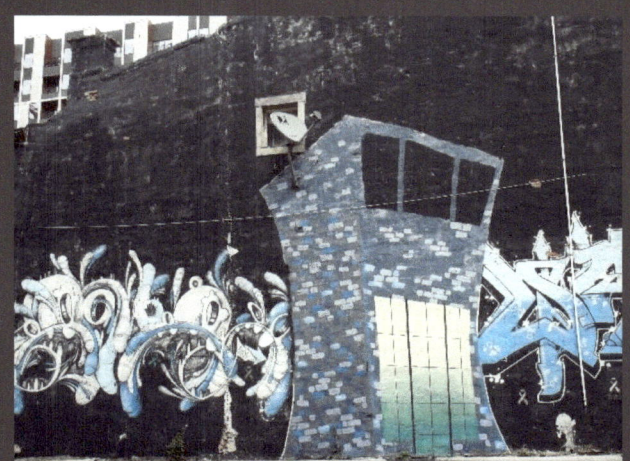
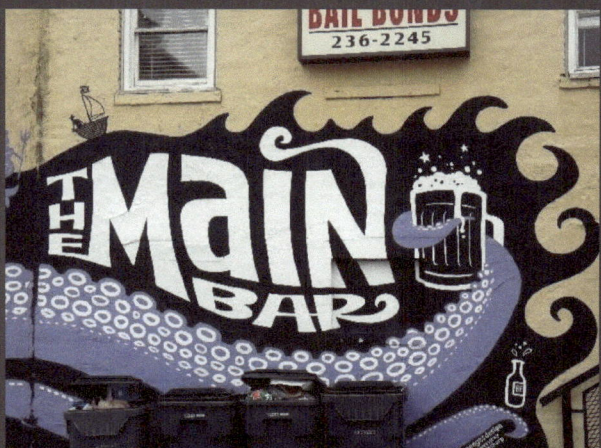

W Rich St Bridge over Scioto River

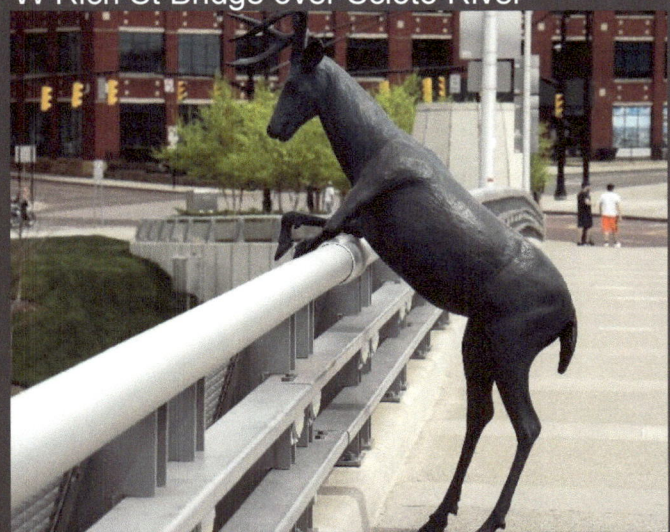
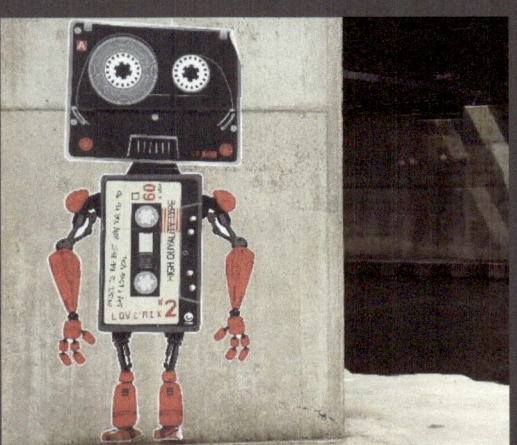

Railway Bridge south of Main street

Topiary Garden Park, E Town St

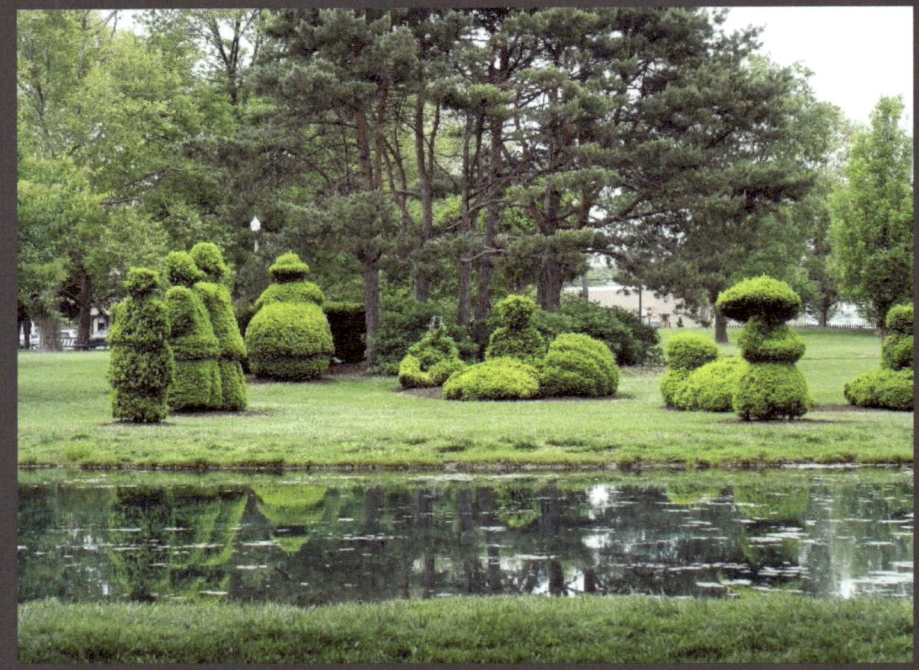

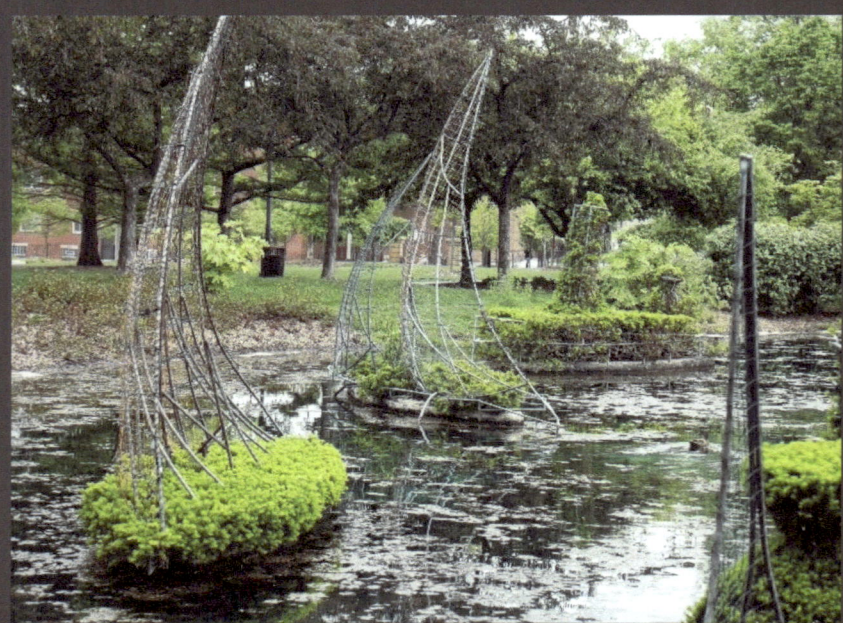

Near Broad and High

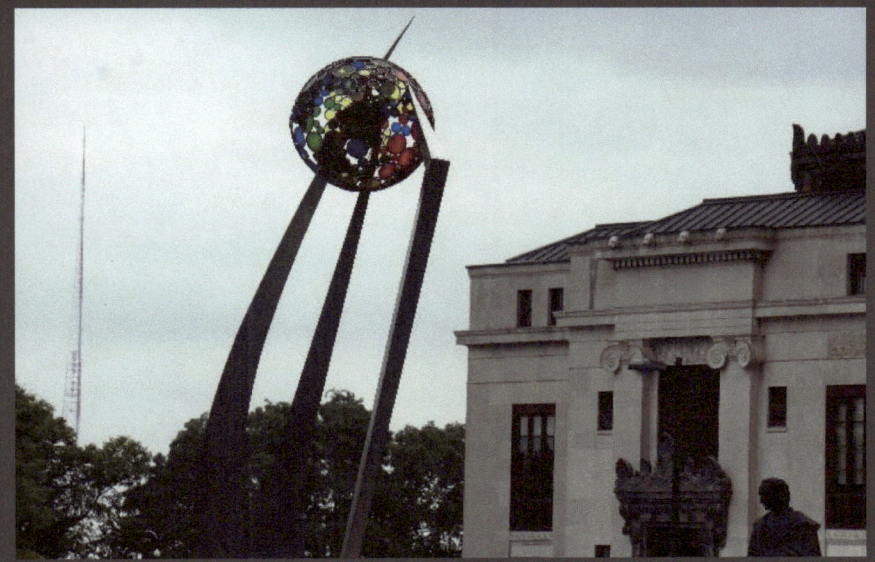

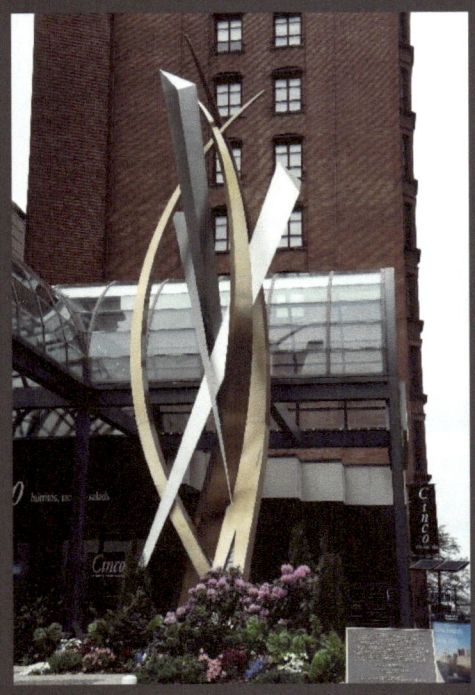

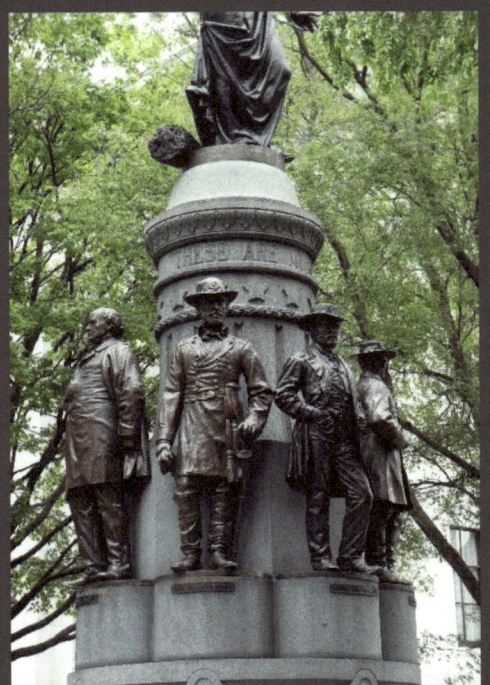

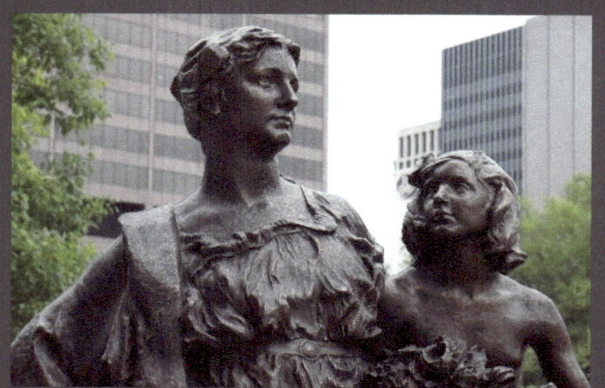

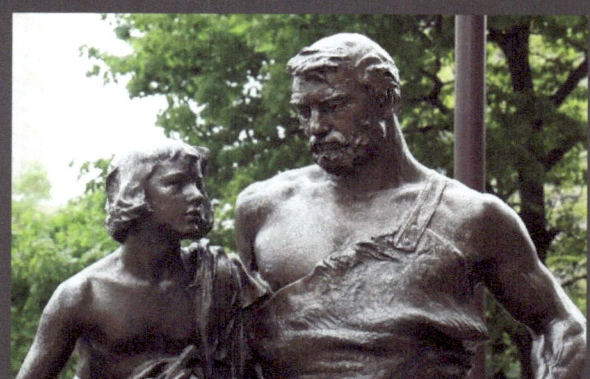

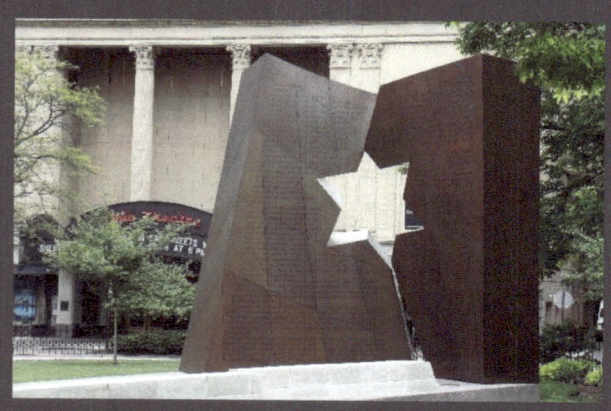

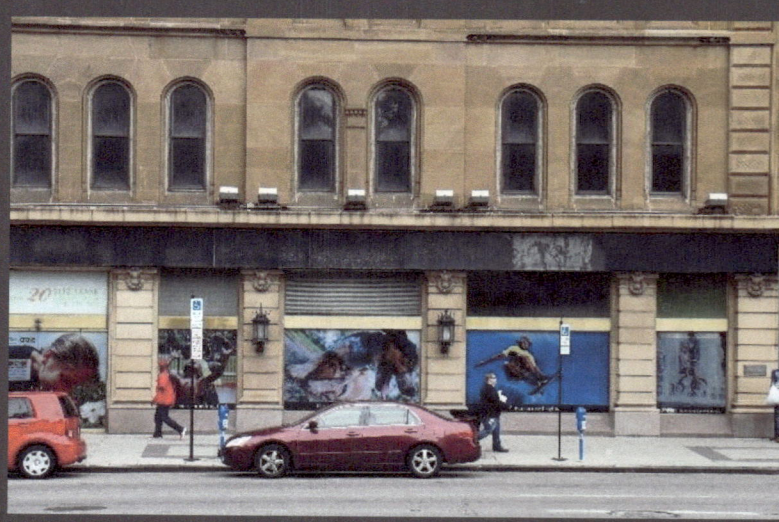

Note card (greeting card) and large print of the photos in this book can be ordered by writing which photos are to be ordered in email to **sn@ismr.us** This service is limited to United State customers only.

 The cost of one note card is $6 (shipping free) including an envelop enclosed in cellophane bag. To order card(s), write in the email the page number of the photo in this book (and which photo if multiple), and how many cards are desired. Any number of photos or cards for each photo can be ordered. An invoice will be returned to which a payment may be done securely by Paypal or credit card. Once the payment is finished it will take about a week until the products are mailed to the customer.

 For large print(s) please send inquiry to **sn@ismr.us**

Cultural Arts in Columbus Book Series

Vol 1 Walking in Short North of Columbus OH

Vol 2 Murals and Street Arts in Columbus OH

   Part 1 Shot North and Downtown

Vol 3 Murals and Street Arts in Columbus OH

   Part 2 Franklinton (Forthcoming soon)